SPECIAL

THE OPEN MEDIA PAMPHLET SERIES

EDITION

THE OPEN MEDIA PAMPHLET SERIES

TERRORISM
Theirs & Ours

EQBAL AHMAD

**Foreword and Interview
by David Barsamian**

Series editor Greg Ruggiero

SEVEN STORIES PRESS / NEW YORK

CONTENTS

ACKNOWLEDGMENTS

The first section of this book, "Terrorism, Theirs &
Ours," is an edited transcript of a public talk Eqbal
Ahmad delivered on October 12, 1998 at the University of Colorado, Boulder. The second section of
this book is an edited excerpt from Eqbal Ahmad:
Confronting Empire, Interviews with David
Barsamian (South End Press, 2000). Special thanks to
the South End Press Collective for their solidarity,
encouragement, and support.

FOREWORD

by David Barsamian

Eqbal Ahmad was one of the major activist scholars of this era. He was born in India probably in 1934. He was never quite sure. He left with his brothers for the newly created state of Pakistan in 1947. In 1996, the BBC did a powerful and moving TV documentary chronicling Ahmad's trek in a refugee caravan from his village in Bihar to Pakistan. The film, not shown on PBS in the U.S., is remarkable not just as an historical document but also for providing insight into the dangers of sectarian nationalism. Ahmad's secular thinking was surely shaped by the wrenching communal and political violence he experienced as a youngster. Even before the subcontinent was engulfed in the homicidal convulsions of 1947, Ahmad witnessed his own father murdered before him.

Ahmad came to the United States in the 1950s to study at Princeton. Later he went to Algeria. It was there that his ideas about national liberation and anti-imperialism crystallized. He worked with Frantz

Fanon, author of *The Wretched of the Earth,* during the revolt against the French. Returning to the U.S., he became active in the civil rights and anti–Vietnam War movements. It was during his involvement in the latter that I first heard his name. He was accused of plotting to kidnap Henry Kissinger. The trumped-up charges were dismissed.

I did my first interview with him in the early 1980s in his apartment on New York's Upper West Side. It was memorable. I had just gotten a new tape recorder. I returned home thinking, Wow, I've got a great interview. I hit play and discovered the tape was blank. I had failed to turn the machine on. With considerable embarrassment I explained to him what happened. He said, "No problem." He invited me over the next day and we did another interview. This time, I pressed the right buttons. Whenever I tell that story, his friends would nod and say, "That's Eqbal."

Ahmad's radical politics and outspoken positions made him a pariah in academic circles. After years of being an intellectual migrant worker, Hampshire College in Amherst, Massachusetts, hired him in the early 1980s as a professor. He taught there until his retirement in 1997. He spent most of his final years in Islamabad where he wrote a weekly column for *Dawn,* Pakistan's oldest English-language newspaper. His political work consisted chiefly of trying to bridge differences with India on the issues of Kashmir and nuclear weapons. He was also speaking out against

EQBAL AHMAD

the rise of Islamic fundamentalism and was concerned about the possible Talibanization of Pakistan.

Eqbal Ahmad died in Islamabad, Pakistan, on May 11, 1999. His close friend Edward Said wrote, "He was perhaps the shrewdest and most original ant-imperialist analyst of the postwar world, particularly of the dynamics between the West and postcolonial Asia and Africa; a man of enormous charisma, dazzling eloquence, incorruptible ideals, unfailing generosity and sympathy.... Whether on the conflict between Israelis and Palestinians or India and Pakistan, he was a force for a just struggle but also for a just reconciliation.... Humanity and genuine secularism...had no finer champion."

"Terrorism: Theirs & Ours" was one of Eqbal Ahmad's last public talks in the United States. He spoke at the University of Colorado at Boulder in October 1998. It was broadcast nationally and internationally on my weekly *Alternative Radio* program. Eqbal Ahmad's near prophetic sense is stunning. After the September 11 terrorist attacks, I aired the speech again. Listeners called in great numbers requesting copies. They almost all believed that the talk had just been recorded.

TERRORISM: THEIRS & OURS

by Eqbal Ahmad

Until the 1930s and early 1940s, the Jewish underground in Palestine was described as "terrorist." Then something happened: around 1942, as news of the Holocaust was spreading, a certain liberal sympathy with the Jewish people began to emerge in the Western world. By 1944, the terrorists of Palestine, who were Zionists, suddenly began being described as "freedom fighters." If you look in history books you can find at least two Israeli prime ministers, including Menachem Begin,* appearing in "Wanted" posters saying, TERRORISTS, REWARD [THIS MUCH]. The highest reward I have seen offered was 100,000 British pounds for the head of Menachem Begin, the terrorist.

From 1969 to 1990, the Palestine Liberation Organization (PLO) occupied center stage as a terrorist organization. Yasir Arafat has been repeatedly described as the "chief of terrorism" by the great sage of American journalism, William Safire of *The New York Times*. On September 29, 1998, I was rather

---

*Yitzhak Shamir is the other.

amused to notice a picture of Yasir Arafat and Israeli prime minister Benjamin Netanyahu standing on either side of President Bill Clinton. Clinton was looking toward Arafat, who looked meek as a mouse. Just a few years earlier, Arafat would appear in photos with a very menacing look, a gun holstered to his belt. That's Yasir Arafat. You remember those pictures, and you'll remember the next one.

In 1985, President Ronald Reagan received a group of ferocious-looking, turban-wearing men who looked like they came from another century. I had been writing about the very same men for *The New Yorker*. After receiving them in the White House, Reagan spoke to the press, referring to his foreign guests as "freedom fighters." These were the Afghan mujahideen. They were at the time, guns in hand, battling the "Evil Empire." For Reagan, they were the moral equivalent of our Founding Fathers.

In August 1998, another American President ordered missile strikes to kill Osama bin Laden and his men in Afghanistan-based camps. Mr. bin Laden, at whom fifteen American missiles were fired to hit in Afghanistan, was only a few years earlier the moral equivalent of George Washington and Thomas Jefferson. I'll return to the subject of bin Laden later.

I am recalling these stories to point out that the official approach to terrorism is rather complicated, but not without characteristics. To begin with, terrorists change. The terrorist of yesterday is the hero of today, and the hero of yesterday becomes the terrorist of today. In a constantly changing world of images, we have to keep our heads straight to know what terrorism is and what it is not. Even more importantly, we need to know what causes terrorism and how to stop it.

Secondly, the official approach to terrorism is a posture of inconsistency, one which evades definition. I have examined at least twenty official documents on terrorism. Not one offers a definition. All of them explain it polemically in order to arouse our emotions, rather than exercise our intelligence. I'll give you an example which is representative. On October 25, 1984, Secretary of State George Shultz gave a long speech on terrorism at the Park Avenue Synagogue in New York City. In the State Department Bulletin of seven single-spaced pages, there is not a single clear definition of terrorism. What we get instead are the following statements. Number one: "Terrorism is a modern barbarism that we call terrorism." Number two is even more brilliant: "Terrorism is a form of political violence." Number three: "Terrorism is a threat to Western civilization." Number four: "Terrorism is a menace to Western moral values." Do these accomplish anything other than arouse emotions? This is typical.

Officials don't define terrorism because definitions involve a commitment to analysis, comprehension, and adherence to some norms of consistency. That's the second characteristic of the official approach to terrorism. The third characteristic is that the absence of definition does not prevent officials from being globalistic. They may not define terrorism, but they can call it a menace to good order, a menace to the moral values of Western civilization, a menace to humankind. Therefore, they can call for it to be stamped out worldwide. Anti-terrorist policies therefore, must be global. In the same speech he gave in New York City, George Shultz also said: "There is no question about our ability to use force where and when it is needed to counter terrorism." There is no geographical limit. On the same day, U.S. missiles struck Afghanistan and Sudan. Those two countries are 2,300 miles apart, and they were hit by missiles belonging to a country roughly 8,000 miles away. Reach is global.

A fourth characteristic is that the official approach to terrorism claims not only global reach, but also a certain omniscient knowledge. They claim to know where terrorists are, and therefore, where to hit. To quote George Shultz again, "We know the difference between terrorists and freedom fighters, and as we look around, we have no trouble telling one from the other." Only Osama bin Laden doesn't know that he was an ally one day and an enemy another. That's very confusing for Osama bin Laden. I'll come back to him toward the end; it's a real story.

Fifth, the official approach eschews causation.

They don't look at why people resort to terrorism. Cause? What cause? Another example: on December 18, 1985, *The New York Times* reported that the foreign minister of Yugoslavia—you remember the days when there was a Yugoslavia—requested the secretary of state of the U.S. to consider the causes of Palestinian terrorism. The secretary of state, George Shultz, and I'm quoting from *The New York Times*, "went a bit red in the face. He pounded the table and told the visiting foreign minister, "There is no connection with any cause. Period." Why look for causes?

A sixth characteristic of the official approach to terrorism is the need for the moral revulsion we feel against terror to be selective. We are to denounce the terror of those groups which are officially disapproved. But we are to applaud the terror of those groups of whom officials do approve. Hence, President Reagan's statement, "I am a contra." We know that the contras of Nicaragua were by any definition terrorists, but the media heed the dominant view.

More importantly to me, the dominant approach also excludes from consideration the terrorism of friendly governments. Thus, the United States excused, among others, the terrorism of Pinochet, who killed one of my closest friends, Orlando Letelier, one of Chilean president Salvador Allende's top diplomats, killed in a car bombing in Washington, DC in 1976. And it excused the terror of Zia ul-Haq, the military dictator of Pakistan, who killed many of my friends there. All I want to tell you is that according to my ignorant calculations, the ratio of people killed by the state terror of Zia ul-Haq, Pinochet, Argentinian, Brazilian, Indonesian type, versus the killing of the PLO and other organizations is literally, conservatively, 1,000 to 1. That's the ratio.

History unfortunately recognizes and accords visibility to power, not to weakness. Therefore, visibility has been accorded historically to dominant groups. Our time—the time that begins with Columbus—has been one of extraordinary unrecorded holocausts. Great civilizations have been wiped out. The Mayas, the Incas, the Aztecs, the American Indians, the Canadian Indians were all wiped out. Their voices have not been heard, even to this day. They are heard, yes, but only when the dominant power suffers, only when resistance has a semblance of costing, of exacting a price, when a Custer is killed or when a Gordon is besieged. That's when you know that there were Indians or Arabs fighting and dying.

My last point on this subject is that during the Cold War period, the United States sponsored terrorist regimes like Somoza in Nicaragua and Batista in Cuba, one after another. All kinds of tyrants have been America's friends. In Nicaragua it was the contra, in Afghanistan, the mujahideen.

Now, what about the other side? What is terrorism? Our first job should be to define the damn thing, name it, give it a description other than "moral equivalent of founding fathers" or "a moral outrage to Western civilization." This is what *Webster's Collegiate Dictionary* says: "Terror is an intense, overpowering fear." Terrorism is "the use of terrorizing methods of governing or resisting a government." This simple definition has one great virtue: it's fair. It focuses on the use of violence that is used illegally, extra-constitutionally, to coerce. And this definition is correct because it treats terror for what it is, whether a government or private group commits it.

Have you noticed something? Motivation is omitted. We're not talking about whether the cause is just or unjust. We're talking about consensus, consent, absence of consent, legality, absence of legality, constitutionality, absence of constitutionality. Why do we keep motives out? Because motives make no difference. In the course of my work I have identified five types of terrorism; state terrorism, religious terrorism (Catholics killing Protestants, Sunnis killing Shiites, Shiites killing Sunnis), criminal terrorism, political terrorism, and oppositional terrorism. Sometimes these five can converge and overlap. Oppositional protest terrorism can become pathological criminal terrorism. State terror can take the form of private terror. For example, we're all familiar with the death squads in Latin America or in Pakistan where the government has employed private people to kill its opponents. It's not quite official. It's privatized. In Afghanistan, Central America, and Southeast Asia, the CIA employed in its covert operations drug pushers. Drugs and guns often go together. The categories often overlap.

Of the five types of terror, the official approach is to focus on only one form—political terrorism— which claims the least in terms of loss of human lives and property. The form that exacts the highest loss is state terrorism. The second highest loss is created by religious terrorism, although religious terror has, relatively speaking, declined. If you are looking historically, however, religious terrorism has caused massive loss. The next highest loss is caused by criminal terrorism. A Rand Corporation study by Brian Jenkins examining a ten-year period (1978 to 1988) showed fifty percent of terrorism was committed without any political cause. No politics. Simply crime and pathology. So the focus is on only one, the political terrorist, the PLO, the bin Laden, whoever you want to take.

Why do they do it? What makes terrorists tick?

I would like to knock out some quick answers. First, the need to be heard. Remember, we are dealing with a minority group, the political, private terrorist. Normally, and there are exceptions, there is an effort to be heard, to get their grievances recognized and addressed by people. The Palestinians, for example, the superterrorists of our time, were dispossessed in 1948. From 1948 to 1968 they went to every court in the world. They knocked on every door. They had been completely deprived of their land, their country, and nobody was listening. In desperation, they invented a new form of terror: the airplane hijacking. Between 1968 and 1975 they pulled the world up by its ears. That kind of terror is a violent way of expressing long-felt grievances. It makes the world hear. It's normally undertaken by small, helpless groupings that feel powerless. We still haven't done the Palestinians justice, but at least we all know they exist. Now, even the Israelis acknowledge. Remember what Golda Meir, prime minister of Israel, said in 1970: There are no Palestinians. They do not exist.

They damn well exist now.

Secondly, terrorism is an expression of anger, of feeling helpless, angry, alone. You feel like you have to hit back. Wrong has been done to you, so you do it. During the hijacking of the TWA jet in Beirut, Judy Brown of Belmar, New Jersey, said that she kept hearing them yell, "New Jersey, New Jersey." What did they have in mind? She thought that they were going after her. Later on it turned out that the terrorists were referring to the U.S. battleship New Jersey, which had heavily shelled the Lebanese civilian population in 1983.[1]

Another factor is a sense of betrayal, which is connected to that tribal ethic of revenge. It comes into the picture in the case of people like bin Laden. Here is a man who was an ally of the United States, who saw America as a friend; then he sees his country being occupied by the United States and feels betrayal. Whether there is a sense of right and wrong is not what I'm saying. I'm describing what's behind this kind of extreme violence.

Sometimes it's the fact that you have experienced violence at other people's hands. Victims of violent abuse often become violent people. The only time when Jews produced terrorists in organized fashion was during and after the Holocaust. It is rather remarkable that Jewish terrorists hit largely innocent people or U.N. peacemakers like Count Bernadotte of Sweden, whose country had a better record on the Holocaust. The men of Irgun, the Stern Gang, and the Hagannah terrorist groups came in the wake of the Holocaust. The experience of victimhood itself produces a violent reaction.

In modern times, with modern technology and means of communications, the targets have been globalized. Therefore, globalization of violence is an aspect of what we call globalization of the economy and culture in the world as a whole. We can't expect everything else to be globalized and violence not to be. We do have visible targets. Airplane hijacking is something new because international travel is relatively new, too. Everybody now is in your gunsight. Therefore the globe is within the gunsight. That has globalized terror.

Finally, the absence of revolutionary ideology has been central to the spread of terror in our time. One of the points in the big debate between Marxism and anarchism in the nineteenth century was the use of terror. The Marxists argued that the true revolutionary does not assassinate. You do not solve social problems by individual acts of violence. Social problems require social and political mobilization, and thus wars of liberation are to be distinguished from terrorist organizations. The revolutionaries didn't reject violence, but they rejected terror as a viable tactic of revolution. That revolutionary ideology has gone out at the moment. In the 1980s and 1990s, revolutionary ideology receded, giving in to the globalized individual. In general terms, these are among the many forces that are behind modern terrorism.

To this challenge rulers from one country after another have been responding with traditional methods. The traditional method of shooting it out, whether it's with missiles or some other means. The Israelis are very proud of it. The Americans are very proud of it. The French became very proud of it. Now the Pakistanis are very proud of it. The Pakistanis say, Our commandos are the best. Frankly, it won't work. A central problem of our time: political minds rooted in the past at odds with modern times, producing new realities.

Let's turn back for a moment to Osama bin Laden. *Jihad*, which has been translated a thousand times as "holy war," is not quite that. *Jihad* in Arabic means "to struggle." It could be struggle by violence or struggle by non-violent means. There are two forms, the small *jihad* and the big *jihad*. The small *jihad* involves external violence. The big *jihad* involves a struggle within oneself. Those are the concepts. The reason I mention it is that in Islamic history, *jihad* as an international violent phenomenon had for all practical purposes disappeared in the last four hundred years. It was revived suddenly with American help in the 1980s. When the Soviet Union intervened in Afghanistan, which borders Pakistan, Zia ul-Haq saw an opportunity and launched a *jihad* there against godless communism. The U.S. saw a God-sent opportunity to mobilize one billion Muslims against what Reagan called the Evil Empire. Money started pouring in. CIA agents starting going all over the Muslim world recruiting people to fight in the great *jihad*. Bin Laden was one of the early prize recruits. He was not only an Arab, he was a Saudi multimillionaire willing to put his own money into the matter. Bin Laden went around recruiting people for the *jihad* against communism.

I first met Osama bin Laden in 1986. He was rec-ommended to me by an American official who may have been an agent. I was talking to the American and asked him who were the Arabs there that would be very interesting to talk with. By *there* I meant in Afghanistan and Pakistan. The American official told me, "You must meet Osama." I went to see Osama. There he was, rich, bringing in recruits from Algeria, from Sudan, from Egypt, just like Sheikh Abdul Rahman, an Egyptian cleric who was among those convicted for the 1993 World Trade Center bombing. At that moment, Osama bin Laden was a U.S. ally. He remained an ally. He turned at a particular moment. In 1990 the U.S. went into Saudi Arabia with military forces. Saudi Arabia is the holy place of Muslims, home of Mecca and Medina. There had never been foreign troops there. In 1990, during the build-up to the Gulf War, they went in in the name of helping Saudi Arabia defend itself. Osama bin Laden remained quiet. Saddam was defeated, but the American foreign troops stayed on in the land of the kaba (the sacred site of Islam in Mecca). Bin Laden wrote letter after letter saying, Why are you here? Get out! You came to help but you have stayed on. Finally he started a *jihad* against the other occupiers. His mission is to get American troops out of Saudi Arabia. His earlier mission was to get Russian troops out of Afghanistan.

A second point to be made about him is that he come from a tribal people. Being a millionaire doesn't matter. His code of ethics is tribal. The tribal code of ethics consists of two words: loyalty and revenge. You are my friend. You keep your word. I am loyal to you. You break your word, I go on my path of revenge. For him, America has broken its word. The loyal friend has betrayed him. Now they're going to go for you. They're going to do a lot more. These are the chickens of the Afghanistan war coming home to roost.

What is my recommendation to America?

First, avoid extremes of double standards. If you're going to practice double standards, you will be paid with double standards. Don't use it. Don't condone Israeli terror, Pakistani terror, Nicaraguan terror, El Salvadoran terror, on the one hand, and then complain about Afghan terror or Palestinian terror. It doesn't work. Try to be even-handed. A superpower cannot promote terror in one place and reasonably expect to discourage terrorism in another place. It won't work in this shrunken world.

Do not condone the terror of your allies. Condemn them. Fight them. Punish them. Avoid covert operations and low-intensity warfare. These are breeding grounds for terrorism and drugs. In the Australian documentary about covert operations, *Dealing with the Demon*, I say that wherever covert operations have been, there is a drug problem. Because the structure of covert operations, Afghanistan, Vietnam, Nicaragua, Central America, etcetera, have been very hospitable to the drug trade. Avoid covert operations. It doesn't help.

Also, focus on causes and help ameliorate them. Try to look at causes and solve problems. Avoid military solutions. Terrorism is a political problem. Seek political solutions. Diplomacy works. Take the example of President Clinton's attack on bin Laden. Did they know what they were attacking? They say they know, but they don't know. At another point, they were trying to kill Qadaffi. Instead, they killed his young daughter. The poor child hadn't done anything. Qadaffi is still alive. They tried to kill Saddam Hussein. Instead they killed Laila bin Attar, a prominent artist, an innocent woman. They tried to kill bin Laden and his men. Twenty-five other people died. They tried to destroy a chemical factory in Sudan. Now they are admitting that they destroyed a pharmaceutical plant that produced half the medicine for Sudan.

Four of the missiles intended for Afghanistan fell in Pakistan. One was slightly damaged, two were totally damaged, one was totally intact. For ten years the American government has kept an embargo on Pakistan because Pakistan was trying, stupidly, to build nuclear weapons and missiles. So the U.S. has a technology embargo on my country. One of the missiles was intact. What do you think the Pakistani official told the *Washington Post*? He said it was a gift from Allah. Pakistan wanted U.S. technology. Now they have the technology, and Pakistan's scientists are examining this missile very carefully. It fell into the wrong hands. Look for political solutions. Military solutions cause more problems than they solve.

Finally, please help reinforce and strengthen the framework of international law. There was a criminal court in Rome. Why didn't the U.S. go there first to get a warrant against bin Laden, if they have some evidence? Enforce the United Nations. Enforce the International Court of Justice. Get a warrant, then go after him internationally.

A CONVERSATION WITH EQBAL AHMAD

This section consists of two interviews that David Barsamian held with Eqbal Ahmad at Hampshire College in Amherst, Massachusetts in December 1996 and August 1998.

THE ISSUE OF KASHMIR

The Indian government steadfastly refuses to acknowledge the right of Kashmiris to self-determination. They say that issue was settled in 1947, when the Maharaja of Kashmir acceded to the Indian Union.

That's the official position of India. Pakistan has a similar one, but with much less lethal effect. The Pakistan government's position is that the Kashmiris were given the right to exercise their self-determination by choosing between India and Pakistan. This right was written into the United Nations Security Council resolution of 1948. So Pakistan is insisting that there should be a referendum or a plebiscite on the basis of the U.N. resolution, which would force the Kashmiris to choose between India and Pakistan.

Fifty years later the Kashmiris are more interested in choosing either maximum autonomy from these two countries or independence from them. Pakistan is not conceding that. The difference in the Pakistani and Indian position is that India is occupying the

Kashmir Valley. There has been a revolt since 1989. Approximately 50,000 people have been killed, mostly at the hands of the Indian military. India's denial is costing lives and property, while Pakistan's old position is not quite as costly but is still outdated. I've been arguing in favor of both India and Pakistan coming to an agreement to give the Kashmiris a chance to decide their future. It can be done in such a way that it does not hurt the interests of either Pakistan or India.

India's Prime Minister Nehru agreed to hold a plebiscite but then never followed through. There were delays and delays and then it never happened.

Under Nehru, India had committed itself to holding a plebiscite and carrying out the U.N. resolution. That promise India has reneged on.

How would you solve the Kashmir problem?

I have argued at some length that India and Pakistan must begin the process of finding a solution with the leaders of the Kashmiri movement. Having said that, we need to recall a little bit of the background. Kashmir, since 1948, has been divided between India and Pakistan. On the Pakistani side is primarily a Punjabi-speaking area which we call Azad Kashmir, "Free Kashmir," with its capital in Muzaffarabad. It has its own autonomous government, and it does exercise autonomy over local matters. Pakistan almost totally controls its foreign policy, defense, and commercial policies. So in a sense its autonomy is very severely compromised.

India controls all of the rest of Kashmir, which divides into three broad parts. There is the valley. Eighty to eighty-five percent of the valley's population is Muslim. They have over the last two centuries suffered great discrimination, injustice, and oppression at the hands of the *maharaja* of Kashmir put in power by the British. Both regimes were genuinely discriminatory, to the point where Muslims were really serfs. They couldn't join any government services. They were not allowed to study. It was very bad. Since 1948, the situation has improved. More Kashmiris have gone to schools and been educated. A sort of Kashmiri nationalism is centered in the valley with its population of about four million. The valley is one identifiable unique component of Kashmir which is the seat of *Kashmiriat,* Kashmiri nationalism, Kashmiri aspirations.

Then you have Ladakh, which is predominantly Buddhist. Some portions of it are Muslim. India considers Ladakh to be terribly important for its defense because it is next to China. Then there is the large district of Jammu, where roughly 60 percent of the population is non-Kashmiri-speaking Hindus. I think their religion is less important than their ethnicity— they are Dogras, the same people as the *maharaja*. They have been favored. They speak a different language, Dogri. They feel much closer to India. They do not share the premises of *Kashmiriat*.

Now keep this division in mind. Kashmir is divided between Pakistan and India. The part under India is the most disputed at the moment. That's where the uprising is, and that divides into three parts: the valley, Ladakh, and Jammu. My proposal is that we seek an agreement which leaves the Pakistani part under Pakistani control. Jammu and Ladakh, which do not share the premises of Kashmiri nationalism, should be left under Indian sovereignty. The valley should be given independence. But the agreement among the three—Kashmiri leadership, Pakistan, and India—must envisage uniting Kashmir with divided sovereignty. Unite the territory, keep sovereignties divided, which in our time is fairly possible. Remove the lines of control, remove border patrols, make trade free among these three, make India, Pakistan, and the independent Kashmiri government jointly responsible for the defense of this mountain area.

Kashmir at the moment is a bone of contention between Pakistan and India on the one hand, Kashmiri nationalism in India on the other hand, between Dogras and Kashmiris on yet another hand, and anxieties and fears among Buddhists and Kashmiris on still yet another hand. My proposal would create, instead of a bone of contention, a bridge of peace. Allow each community maximum autonomy with divided sovereignty.

Kashmir would then serve as the starting point of normalizing relations between India and Pakistan. And if India and Pakistan normalize relations, with free trade, free exchange of professionals, and reduction in arms spending, in ten years we will start looking like East Asia. We are competing with each other with so little money. Four hundred million people in India out of a population of 950 million are living below the poverty line.... This condition has to be removed.

Do you think the resolution of the Kashmir dispute could provide that opening to heal the wounds between Pakistan and India?

They can reach agreements on more important issues than Kashmir. Kashmir is more of an emotional issue.

The division of water—of rivers—was a much more central issue, because that's the lifeline of Pakistan and of the Indian part of Punjab and Haryana. But we reached an agreement on water, the 1960 Indus Basin Water Treaty, years ago, and we have honored it. The World Bank played a very central role in bringing about the treaty, one of the few good things that the World Bank has ever done. Today we are not fighting over water any more. In 1996, India and Bangladesh reached a water agreement on the Ganges.[2]

Except for the die-hard Hindu nationalists in India and the militant Islamic parties in Pakistan, there is no rancor among secular people or among common people between India and Pakistan. In fact, the longer we delay normalization of relations between India and Pakistan and the resolution of the Kashmir conflict, the more we are creating an environment for the spread of Islamic and Hindu militancy.

ISLAMIC FUNDAMENTALISM AND U.S. FOREIGN POLICY

Media coverage of Islamic fundamentalism seems to be very selective. There are certain types that are not discussed at all. For example, the Saudi version, which may be among the most extreme. Americans hear a lot about Hezbollah and Hamas and groups in Egypt, like the Akhwan, the Muslim brotherhood.

This is a very interesting matter you are raising.... Saudi Arabia's Islamic government has been by far the most fundamentalist in the history of Islam. Even today, for example, women drive in Iran. They can't drive in Saudi Arabia. Today, for example, men and women are working in offices together in Iran. Women wear chador, but they work in offices. In Saudi Arabia, they cannot do it. So on the basis of the nature and extent of fundamentalist principles or right-wing ideology, Saudi Arabia is much worse in practice than Iran. But it has been the ally of the United States since 1932, so nobody has questioned it.

But much more than that is involved. Throughout

the Cold War, starting in 1945 when it inherited its role as a world power, the United States has seen militant Islam as a counterweight to communist parties in the Muslim world. During this entire period, the Muslim brotherhood in Egypt was not an enemy of the United States. The U.S. government actually promoted and supported the Islamic regime that is now in power in Sudan. General Muhammad Gaafar al-Nimeiry was allied to the Islamic movement of Sudan, and was a friend.

America's two major leverages on its allies in Western Europe and Asia—the nuclear umbrella and economic superiority—had drastically diminished by the early 1970s. The U.S. was looking for new leverages over its allies. They picked the Middle East because this was where the energy resources for the industrial economies of Japan and Europe came from. An established, unchallenged American influence in this region could control prices and show Europe and Japan, "We can give you cheap oil. We can make your oil expensive. We hold your economic lifeline."

This was the time of the Nixon Doctrine, namely, the use of regional powers to police the region for the United States. In the Middle East, they chose Iran and Israel. In the Pentagon, throughout most of the 1970s, they were called "our two eyes in the Middle East." In 1978, after having or perhaps because of having taken some $20 billion of military hardware from the United States, the shah of Iran fell under the weight of his own militarization. The 1979 Islamic revolution threatened American interests deeply, materializing in an uglier form during the hostage crisis. Within a year, quite ironically, something totally the opposite happens. The Soviet Union intervened in Afghanistan. In Pakistan, an Islamic fundamentalist dictator promoted, with the help of the CIA, an Islamic fundamentalist resistance against the Soviets in Afghanistan. Now what you had was Islamic fundamentalists of a really hardcore variety, the *mujahideen* in Afghanistan, taking on the "Evil Empire." They received billions in arms between 1981 and 1988 from the United States alone. Add additional support from Saudi Arabia, under American encouragement. American operatives went about the Muslim world recruiting for the *jihad* in Afghanistan, because the U.S. saw it as an opportunity to mobilize the Muslim world against communism. That opportunity was exploited by recruiting *mujahideen* in Algeria, Sudan, Egypt, Yemen, and Palestine. From everywhere they came. They received training from the CIA. They received arms from the CIA. I have argued in some of my writings that the notion of *jihad* as "just struggle" had not existed in the Muslim world since the tenth century until the United States revived it during its *jihad* against the Soviet Union in Afghanistan.

Since then, almost every Islamic militant, including those in Israel, Algeria, and Egypt...has been trained in Afghanistan. The CIA calls it "Islamic blowback."

These are aspects that the American media are not willing to touch on. *The New York Times'* four foreign affairs columnists are neither qualified nor would they want to be qualified to comment on these realities.

PAKISTAN AND U.S. FOREIGN POLICY

What side effects have U.S. support of the mujahideen had on Pakistani society?

One is the extraordinary proliferation of drugs and guns. Something like $10 billion in arms was pumped into Pakistan and Afghanistan. Half of it at least rebounded and became part of international trade. Much of it ended up in Pakistan. So, you have a situation in Pakistan where almost every third man is armed...with automatic weapons, Kalishnikovs, and grenade launchers. What used to be small crimes have now become big crimes, because petty thieves are armed with weapons that can lead to killings if they feel threatened. In 1979, at the advent of the Afghanistan revolution, there were an estimated 110,000 drug addicts in Pakistan, mostly addicted to opium, some to hashish. Today, we have 5 million addicts. Opium has become a big trade through Pakistan. It comes from Afghanistan and Iran. We have an estimated $4 billion trade in

Afghan drugs. In a country whose total foreign exports were $6 billion before all this, you introduce $4 billion in trade in drugs. We have created in Pakistan an entire class of rich drug dealers who are paying off this politician here, that bureaucrat there, that port authority there. The political system of the whole country has become enmeshed with the drug mafia. It is not quite as bad as Colombia yet. But it's very close to it.

The third effect is probably the most serious. Pakistan is a very heterogenous society. There are six ethnic groups living together with a combination of antagonism and collaboration. The antagonism consists of something like, "You speak Baluch. I speak Urdu. Our children play together. They have quarreled with each other. My child has beaten your child. We get into an argument over whose child was worse." Previously, it was an argument. Today, bullets can fly. So what used to be, because of ethnic differences in our society, completely minor, local, street arguments, are now made with guns. After a while these little things can accumulate and create ethnic warfare.

Are there any progressive political formations in Pakistan?

At this point, no, except in the nonpolitical and informal sector. The primary expressions of progressive formations in Pakistan today are in the media. Since

1987, we have had freedom of the press. It's very lively. In fact, I think I could say without doubt that the Pakistani press today is probably the liveliest in the third world. It's livelier than in India, Egypt, or Indonesia. My articles come out every week. Women are publishing.

The progressive presence is visible in the women's movement. Zia ul-Haq's military regime, which was supported by the United States, was very harsh on women. It passed a number of anti-women ordinances, including the *hudood* ordinances, which reduced women's witness in court cases to half of a man's witness. *Qisas* ordinances ruled that if a woman was murdered by a man, the murder could be compensated for, by paying money. Blood money justifies the murder of a woman.

The first major resistance came from the Women's Action Forum. Ten thousand women came out in the street and the regime took some fright. The police struck them and beat them up. That's when people generally turned against the military. It looked like it must have been a very weak regime to be beating up women. Women have remained very active. Feminism is the most progressive force in Pakistan today.

Various nongovernmental organizations (NGOs) working on the environment, on protection of land, and against large dams supported by the World Bank are having a political impact. But as a political force, progressivism, for the time being, is dormant.

To what extent did Prime Minister Benazir Bhutto contribute to that? She's seen as modern, English-speaking, educated, and progressive. That's the conventional media image.

She was the first Muslim woman prime minister in world history. Educated at Harvard, Radcliffe, and Oxford, where she was elected the president of the Oxford Union, she's articulate. She's an attractive and courageous woman. She fought the military dictatorship after her father was executed by Zia ul-Haq. She went to prison and lived in house arrest. She lived in exile. So she underwent the gamut of political resistance, oppression, and suffering.

The people of Pakistan rewarded her by electing her prime minister in 1988. As prime minister she proved to be inexperienced, unsuccessful, confused, directionless, and in some respects misguided. The big bureaucrats, army officers, and vested interests moved against her, and her government fell in 1990. People felt that the vested interests were unjust to her. After all, she was very young. She needed to learn, and they didn't give her enough time.

In 1993, the country elected her again. She made those same mistakes and more. She and her husband, Asif Zardari, turned out to be almost unbelievably corrupt, with bribery, payoffs, bank loans to her supporters, patronage untrammeled. Worse, the corruption was not accompanied by production.

The post–Civil War U.S. government was very cor-

rupt. Former Presidents Ulysses S. Grant and
Andrew Johnson could have been indicted, but they
were productive. They were capitalist thieves.

What we have learned in Pakistan is that traditional feudal thieves are much worse than capitalist
ones. They don't even produce. They create no wealth
at all, not even for themselves. They just steal. That's
what Ms. Bhutto did.

THE TALIBAN

***Moving to Afghanistan and the evolving situation
there. The Taliban movement, you suggest in an article, has connections with not just Pakistan but also
with the United States.***

Afghanistan has suffered criminal neglect at the
hands of the United States and its media. In 1979 and
1980, when the Afghan people started resisting Soviet
intervention, the whole of America and Europe mobi-
lized on their side. For the media, it was such a big
story that CBS paid money to stage a battle that it
could broadcast as an exclusive. Afghanistan was in
the news every day. It disappeared from the news the
day the Soviets withdrew. Then, Afghanistan was
abandoned by the media, by the American government, by American academics, and as a result by the
American people. The Afghans who fought the West's
battle with the West's money and with the West's
arms, and in the process distorted themselves, dis-

torted Pakistan, and contributed to the demise of the Soviet Union, found themselves totally abandoned after the Cold War. The Taliban's rise takes place in that vacuum.

The Afghan *mujahideen* fell to fighting with each other. They were all both warriors and drug smugglers. They were known to the CIA as drug smugglers. There were ten factions shooting at each other, when something new develops. The Soviet Union falls apart. Its constituent republics become independent. Among those are the six Soviet republics of Central Asia: Uzbekistan, Kazakhstan, Turkmenistan, Tajikistan, Kirghizstan, and Azerbaijan. These six Central Asian republics, whose majority populations are Muslim, are very close to or bordering on Afghanistan, and also happen to be oil- and natural gas–rich states. So far their resources have passed through the Soviet Union, but now a new game starts: How is this oil and gas going to go out to the world? At this point, American corporations move in.

The American corporations want, obviously, to get hold of the oil and gas. After the Cold War, who controls which resource at whose expense and at what price? Corporations like Texaco, Amoco, and Unocal start going into Central Asia to get hold of these oil and gas fields. But how are they going to get the oil and gas out? Through Turkey and via Afghanistan to Pakistan are two possibilities. Iran is the third, but they don't want to put any pipelines in Iran because Iran is an adversary of America. Therefore, Pakistan and Afghanistan become the places through which they are likely to take pipelines. And then they can cut the Russians out.

President Clinton made personal telephone calls to the presidents of Uzbekistan, Kazakhstan, Tajikistan, and Azerbaijan, urging them to sign pipeline contracts that together amount to billions. These pipelines would go through Turkey and via Afghanistan to Pakistan and take oil to the tankers that would meet them at the ports. The pipeline would go through Afghanistan. Both Pakistan and the United States pick the most murderous, by far the most crazy of Islamic fundamentalist groups, the Taliban, to ensure the safety of the pipelines.

Why would the U.S. support what you describe as the most crazy, most anti-women, most fundamentalist formation in Afghanistan to advance their geopolitical interests? Were not other groups available?

These were deemed the most reliable, perhaps for good reason. In Afghanistan, there are four major ethnic groups. There are the Uzbeks who live in the northern region, near Uzbekistan. There are the Hazaras. They are Persian-speaking, among whom Iran would exercise influence. Therefore, they are not totally reliable. The Tajiks are also Persian-speaking. They have been under Russian influence, but since they are Persian-speaking, Iranian influence on them is potentially strong.

The Taliban come from the Pashtun ethnic grouping. They are the majority people. They have a large presence in Pakistan, where we have something like 15 million Pashtuns. Pakistan has been an old ally of the United States. Its loyalties have been tested. It's much better to have the pipelines under the control of people upon whom the government of Pakistan can exercise some influence, upon whom Iran will have no influence.

The Pashtuns are Sunnis. The Tajiks are partially Shiias, partially Sunnis. The Hazaras are entirely Shiia. The Uzbeks are Sunnis, but their loyalties are divided. They have never been tested. So there are a lot of ethnic considerations, ethnic politics, and historical ties involved.

The U.S. concern is not who is fundamentalist and who is progressive, who treats women nicely and who treats them badly. That's not the issue. The issue is who is more likely to ensure the safety of the oil resources that the United States or its corporations could control?

One of the leaders of the Afghan resistance against the Soviet occupation was Gulbuddin Hekmatyar. His name has been consistently linked with gun running and drug smuggling. Do you have any information on him?

I met him several times. I don't think he is worse

than anyone else. He's a bit more of a killer. He is also more progressive, more modern, much more sensible towards women, for example, than the Taliban.

The Taliban is as retrograde a group as you can find. Their power base is Qandahar, a southern province of Afghanistan. Last year, I spent two weeks there. One day, I heard drums and noises outside the house where I was staying. I rushed out to see what was going on. In this ruined bazaar, destroyed by bombs and fighting from the war, there was a young boy. He couldn't have been more than twelve. His head was shaved. There was a rope around his neck. He was being pulled by that rope in the bazaar. There was a man behind him with a drum. The man slowly beat the drum, dum, dum, dum. The boy was being dragged through the street. I asked, "What has he done?" People said he was caught red-handed. I thought, This is a twelve-year-old kid. What could he have been doing? They said, "He was caught red-handed playing ball." I said, "What kind of ball?" "A tennis ball." "What's wrong with that?" "It's forbidden."

I went off to interview one of the Taliban leaders. He said, "We have forbidden playing ball by boys." I asked why. He said, "Because when boys are playing ball it constitutes undue temptation to men." The same logic that makes them lock up women behind veils and behind walls makes them prevent boys from playing games. It's that kind of madness.

Another time I found the watchman where I was staying literally weeping and very agitated. I asked, "What happened to you?" He said, "They took my radio." I said, "What the hell were you doing? Why did they take your radio?" He said, "I was listening to a singer." Music is banned under the Taliban. People who will ban music and play are, I would say, fifty light years behind the Iranian Islamic regime.

INDIA'S MUSLIM POPULATION

What about the state and condition, both materially as well as psychologically, of India's vast Muslim population? Few people know that, after Indonesia, India has the largest Muslim population in the world. What about their sense of belonging, particularly in this atmosphere of communalism?

It's an interesting question. I think the Indian Muslim identity was very much shaken by the partition of India in 1947. It was deeply shaken because many of them sympathized with Pakistan and its creation. Many of them became confused about what partition means and who they are. Surprisingly, fifty years later, and this may be a great achievement of Nehru and Gandhi's secular ideals, the Indian Muslim feels quite Indian—insecure on grounds of being a Muslim, especially because of the rise of these Hindu fundamentalists, but Indian, not alien, not different, not an outsider, not somebody who should think of going away somewhere. There's a saying in Urdu that translates roughly as "Here is where we will receive our rewards and punishment. This is where we will be until the day of judgment." They have a sense of Indianness. When I went back for the BBC documentary, I sensed that much more. It's very different from the Arabs in Israel and the occupied territories. They don't feel Israeli. They don't feel they have been taken into the state, that they belong to it. The Indian Muslim feels that he's Indian, and he's going to bloody well stand up and fight for it. That's an important achievement of the Indian National Congress and the leadership of Gandhi and Nehru, I think, which people are not willing to recognize. It's an important achievement also of that Muslim leadership which has stayed in India, which opposed the idea of Pakistan, people like Abdul Kalam Azad.

But that leadership also included teachers and Muslim clerics.

It included all the Islamic scholars, the *ulema,* of India and Pakistan. In fact, by and large, the *ulema* did not support the Pakistan movement. Ironic, but it's true. Just as the greatest Judaic scholars in the 1920s and 1930s did not support the Zionist movement. They thought it was inimical to the notion of Judaism, to the universal idea of being a Jew.

MUSLIM FUNDAMENTALISM
AND THEOCRACY

But today in Pakistan the Muslim fundamentalist parties are decidedly nationalist, wouldn't you say?

I don't think they can be called "nationalist." They are decidedly Islamist. They are out to capture state power. In that sense they are nationalist; however, they are not quite nationalists in the sense that we use the word. They are pan-Islamists.

They wish to establish a theocratic state?

They wish to establish a theocratic state in Pakistan as the first step toward theocratic states elsewhere. They are part of a generalized theocratic movement in the Muslim world today, which was given a massive push and an armed character by the efforts of the United States in Afghanistan. What happened in Afghanistan has not been discussed in the West. When the Soviet Union intervened in Afghanistan, the U.S. saw in it an opportunity that was twofold. One, they hoped to tie up the Soviet Union in a Vietnam-like war in Afghanistan itself. Two, which becomes more important later on, they saw an opportunity to mobilize the entire Muslim world in a violent way against the Soviet Union, against communism. In an effort to mobilize the entire Muslim world against the "Evil Empire," the CIA started supporting the flow of volunteers from all around the world to fight in Afghanistan, to be socialized into the ideology of anti-communism, and to be trained to hit communists wherever they found them. That's how the militants were recruited and flown in. I have seen planeloads of them arriving from Algeria, Sudan, Saudi Arabia, Egypt, Jordan, even from Palestine, where at that time Israel was supporting Hamas against Al Fatah, Yasir Arafat's faction of the PLO. These people were brought in, given an ideology, and told that armed struggle is virtuous—and the whole notion of *jihad* as an international, pan-Islamic terrorist movement was born. The U.S. has spent billions in producing the bin Ladens of our time. In 1986, I visited the camp they hit in Zhwahar, Afghanistan, in 1998. It was a CIA-sponsored camp. Even after the Soviets withdrew from Afghanistan, the United States did not withdraw its support from bin Laden and others. They continued their support. The Soviet Union collapses in 1990. From 1991, you see a new phenomenon. The United States broke faith with a lot of these people. Promises that were made were broken. Help that was being given was withdrawn. Worse, the United States first moved in on the issue of drugs. Afghanistan and Pakistan had become the largest centers of the drug trade in the 1980s. Many of these people who were supported by the CIA were also engaged in the drug trade. Now the United States did not need them. So it started pressuring the government of Pakistan and the government of Saudi Arabia to clamp down on these groups that were previously working with the United States. They suffered from a double betrayal. There was a failure to continue to fulfill promises made, and there was a turning on old friends.

Who are these people? The majority are tribal. Osama bin Laden comes from the bin Laden clan. Ramzi Yousef is an Afghan-trained fellow. Aimal Kansi is a Baluch tribal.

Ramzi Yousef was identified with the 1993 World Trade Center bombing.

Aimal Kansi has been convicted of killing two CIA agents. Bin Laden is the Saudi millionaire who is alleged to be behind the United States embassy bombings in Kenya and Tanzania in 1998. Ramzi Yousef is of uncertain origin, probably a Pakistani. He grew up in Oman and then came to fight in Afghanistan. But they are all Afghanistan-connected, CIA-connected people. They are also tribal people with a code. Two words are central to that code: loyalty and revenge. The tribal system works around the notion of loyalty and revenge. When your friend to whom you are loyal has betrayed you, you will take revenge. These people have enough of a grudge now on the basis of having been loyal and having been betrayed, number one. Number two, they have been socialized, trained, and equipped to carry on a war of terror against foreign occupiers, which was the Soviet

Union in Afghanistan. Now when they see their lands occupied by the United States, as bin Laden does, it raises a different issue. Bin Laden is merely carrying out the mission to which he committed earlier. Now he is carrying it out against America, because America, from his point of view, is occupying his land.

U.S. UNILATERALISM

The U.S. missile attack on Sudan and Afghanistan is eerily reminiscent of attacks on other countries over the last few decades in this ongoing war against terrorism. There's the now-familiar routine and rhetoric, the high administration officials and generals with their maps, pointers, and satellite photos of the targets. The cast of characters keeps changing but there seems to be something constant among Abu Nidal, Muammar Qadaffi, Saddam Hussein, the PLO, and now bin Laden. They are the incarnation of evil and demons which must be exorcised.

That's understandable, isn't it? The pattern repeats itself continuously. The real questions are really: what is it doing to the world, to the United States? What kind of international system is emerging from it? All the images that you have just described are associated with the Cold War. The Cold War is over, but the phenomenon continues. Interventions go on. What does it mean? What does it mean in terms of political culture in the United States? What does it mean in terms of the insecurities that relatively weaker nations feel in our time? What does it mean for international institutions such as the United Nations and the U.N. Charter? What does it mean for such institutions as the International Court of Justice?

What is remarkable in this period is that the United States is acting unilaterally and declaring its right to act unilaterally when it is the superpower that has access, in some cases controlling access, to international institutions. Why did it not go to the court in Rome and present to it the evidence, on a secret basis if they so wished, that it had against the camp in Afghanistan and against bin Laden and his connection to the factory in Khartoum? There is a fundamental principle of politics, which is that when power has no countervailing forces balancing and checking it, it is always abused. It's abused in extreme ways. The most dangerous characteristic of the current period is that a single power dominates the world militarily and dominates international institutions of peacekeeping and law without countervailing forces. That makes the current world system much more dangerous, especially for the weak and the poor, than even during the Cold War. We are in a time much worse than the Cold War.

You're not suggesting that the prospect of nuclear annihilation which was present in the Cold War is similar to the current situation.

The prospect of nuclear holocaust has probably been marginally reduced, only in the sense that the threat of the Soviet Union and the United States blowing each other up is not there. But the threat of nuclear war in all other areas remains. Nuclear weapons remain. The possibility of misuse of those weapons remains. The possibility of accidents remains. Miscalculations remain. Proliferation remains. There is now no balancing mechanism in the uses and misuses of power. All modern systems of government have been built on the notion that checks and balances are essential to the responsible exercise of power. At the moment, in the international system, there are no checks, no balances, formal or informal, and that makes it more dangerous.

THE LEXICON OF TERRORISM

Dawn, *the English-language newspaper in Pakistan that you write a weekly column for, discussed this very issue of unilateral action in a unipolar world, writing in an August 23, 1998, editorial, "Who will define the parameters of terrorism, or decide where terrorists lurk? Why, none other than the United States, which from the rooftops of the world sets out its claim to be sheriff, judge and hangman, all at one and the same time."[3]*

That's exactly true. Because in a different way than what I was saying earlier, it totally violates the current international system. It stands against the fundamental principle of justice. It's a single power that claims to be judge, accuser, and executioner. You don't allow that in your system. We don't allow it in our system. But we are allowing it on a world scale. Take the case of the missile attack. There is increasing evidence now that the pharmaceutical factory which was hit in Khartoum, Sudan, was not producing any chemical weapons or any weapons of mass destruction. The U.S. government claimed that its intelligence says that it was. But if there is anything that distinguishes the intelligence of the United States, or any other country, it is the number of times they are wrong. A British manager who worked at the factory until last year says there is nothing that could possibly be used for weapons. A foreign cameraman who has filmed the factory says nothing could be seen.[4]

You wrote an article some years ago called "Comprehending Terror" in which you said it's important to start by defining the terminology.[5]

First of all, I think terrorism should be defined in terms of the illegal use of violence for the purposes of influencing somebody's behavior, inflicting punishment, or taking revenge. If we define terror in that way, the first thing we discover is that it has been practiced on a larger scale, globally, both by governments and by private groups. Private groups fall into various categories. The political terrorist is only one category out of many others. When we talk about terror, then, we are talking about the political variety. When we talk about the political variety, the first thing to ask is, what are its roots? Who is the terrorist?

The official attitude toward terror suffers from a suspension of any inquiry into causation. We seldom ask what produces terrorism. There is no connection, said Secretary of State George Shultz, with any cause. Terrorism is just a bad crime. Official definitions, even academic definitions of terror, exclude the illegal violence: torture, burning of villages, destruction of entire peoples, genocide, as outside of the definition of terror, which is to say the bias of terror is against people and in favor of governments. The reality is that the ratio of human losses between official and terrorist activity has been one to a thousand. For every life lost by unofficial terrorism, a thousand have been lost by the official variety.

Another characteristic that we have seen of terror in our time, if you take my definition of it, is that there was a rise of fascist governments in third-world countries, particularly throughout the 1970s and 1980s. All these fascist governments—in Indonesia, Zaire, Iran, South Korea, and elsewhere—were fully supported by one or the other of the superpowers. They have committed a huge amount of terrorist violence, the source of which is the state. Again, there has been very little focus on this by governments, the media, and even academics.

Religious zealotry has been a major source of terror. Terrorist activity is associated almost solely with Islamic groupings. No focus is given to terrorist activities of other religious groupings. It's a global problem. Jewish terrorists have been terrorizing an entire people in the Middle East, with the support of the government of Israel, which is supported by the government of the United States. That terror has included killing people, destroying homes and shooting children, including shooting worshippers in a mosque. The latter happened in Hebron. There's very little focus on terrorism of other religions like Judaism, or for that matter, Hinduism. These people have committed murders and massacres after massacres. They have committed crimes against humanity in the name of religion. Again, our focus, our attention, is uni-focal, on the Islamic variety, not on the Christian, Jewish, Hindu, or Buddhist variety. In other words, it's a parcelized approach to terror.

During the period of the embassy bombings in East Africa and the U.S. attack on Sudan and Afghanistan, the media reported that terrorist formations have "mutated." Whereas before, as you suggest, organizations like the PLO, the Red Brigades in Germany, the Basque-separatist ETA in Spain, and the IRA were much more politically driven, today it's religious-driven groups—therefore more irrational and, by extension, more dangerous.

I am not sure that they are necessarily more irrational. You will allow me a certain dissenting voice on the left from the left also. One of my biggest problems early, it started in 1968, with the PLO was that I kept arguing with them that the violence they were practicing was a violence of the oppressed, but it was not revolutionary violence. It fundamentally lacked the content of revolutionary violence. It had no mobilizing content to it. It was just not morally or politically rooted. It was psychologically and sociologically not selective. It was more an expression of a feeling than an expression of a program. Quite frankly, I feel now that after twenty-five years of being critical toward them, my point of view has been upheld by history. The PLO was not a revolutionary organization. It was an organization of the oppressed, carrying on nonrevolutionary tactics with a nonrevolutionary program by a nonrevolutionary organization. The same is true of the Red Brigades.

The IRA is a different fish. It has swum in a different sea. That's why it has lasted as long as it has and that's why it brought the United States and Britain to the negotiation table, which the PLO did not. The PLO went to surrender. The most tragic point about the PLO is that Israel has not accepted its surrender.

David Anderson of the School of Oriental and African Studies in London comments that this battle will be a "long, perhaps never-ending, attritional war. Pandora's box has been opened, and it won't be closed again," discussing this issue of retaliation, counter-retaliation, an eye for an eye.[6]

I don't see anything as historically permanent. Nothing in history has been permanent. Frankly, I don't think American power is permanent. It itself is very temporary, and therefore its excesses are impermanent and reactions to those excesses have to be, by definition, impermanent. If Anderson means the next five years, then he's right. If he means the next fifty, he may not be right. America is a troubled country, for too many reasons. One is that its economic capabilities do not harmonize with its military capabilities. The second is that its ruling class's will to dominate is not quite shared by its people's will to dominate.

You have recently said that "Osama bin Laden is a sign of things to come." What do you mean by that?

The United States has sowed in the Middle East and in South Asia very poisonous seeds. These seeds are growing now. Some have ripened, and others are ripening. An examination of why they were sown, what has grown, and how they should be reaped is needed. Missiles won't solve the problem.

NOTES

1 John Kifner, "Hijacking of Flight 847: A Grisly Account," *New York Times*, June 17, 1985, p. A10.

2 See Arun P. Elhance, "From War to Water Pacts In Turbulent South Asia," *Christian Science Monitor*, January 15, 1997, p. 19.

3 "Unilateral Muscle-Flexing in a Unipolar World," *Dawn* 52: 227 (August 23, 1998): 15. See Eqbal Ahmad, "Missile Diplomacy," *The Nation* 267: 8 (September 21, 1998): 29.

4 See, for example, James Risen, "To Bomb Sudan Plant, or Not: A Year Later, Debates Rankle," *New York Times*, October 27, 1999, p. A1.

5 Eqbal Ahmad, "Comprehending Terror," *Middle East Report* 16: 3 (May–June 1986): 3–5.

6 David M. Anderson, quoted in Philip Shenon, "Hitting Home: America Takes on a Struggle with Domestic Costs," *New York Times*, August 23, 1998, p. 4:1.

FOR MORE INFORMATION

SOUTH END PRESS
7 Brookline Street, #1
Cambridge, MA 02139
www.southendpress.org
email: southend@southendpress.org

ALTERNATIVE RADIO
2129 Mapleton Drive
Boulder, CO 80304
www.alternativeradio.org
email: ar@orci.com

EQBAL AHMAD was Professor Emeritus of International Relations and Middle Eastern Studies at Hampshire College in Amherst, Massachusetts. Ahmad, who died in 1999, for many years served as managing editor of the quarterly *Race and Class*. His essays appeared in *The Nation* and other journals throughout the world. He wrote a weekly column for *Dawn*, Pakistan's oldest English-language newspaper. *Confronting Empire*, the book of Eqbal Ahmad interviews by David Barsamian, is published by South End Press.

DAVID BARSAMIAN is the founder and director of Alternative Radio, the award-winning Boulder, Colorado–based syndicated weekly broadcast heard all over the world. He is a regular contributor to *The Progressive* and *Z*. His interview books with Noam Chomsky, Howard Zinn, and Edward Said have sold in the the hundreds of thousands. His most recent book with Chomsky is *Propaganda and the Public Mind*. Barsamian's latest book is *The Decilne and Fall of Public Broadcasting*. Both are published by South End Press.

THE PROGRESSIVE GUIDE TO ALTERNATIVE
MEDIA AND ACTIVISM
Project Censored
128 pages / $10.00 / ISBN: 1-888363-84-3

THE UMBRELLA OF U.S. POWER
Noam Chomsky
80 pages / $5.95 / ISBN: 1-888363-85-1

MICRORADIO AND DEMOCRACY:
(LOW) POWER TO THE PEOPLE
Greg Ruggiero
64 pages / $5.95 / ISBN: 1-58322-000-3

POEMS FOR THE NATION:
A COLLECTION OF CONTEMPORARY
POLITICAL POEMS
Allen Ginsberg, with Eliot Katz and Andy Clausen
80 pages / $5.95 / ISBN: 1-58322-012-7

THE CASE AGAINST LAME DUCK
IMPEACHMENT
Bruce Ackerman
80 pages / $8.00 / ISBN: 1-58322-004-6

ACTS OF AGGRESSION:
POLICING "ROGUE" STATES
Noam Chomsky with Edward W. Said
64 pages / $6.95 / ISBN: 1-58322-005-4

THE LAST ENERGY WAR:
THE BATTLE OVER UTILITY DEREGULATION
Harvey Wasserman
80 pages / $5.95 / ISBN: 1-58322-017-8

IT'S THE MEDIA, STUPID
John Nichols and Robert W. McChesney
128 pages / $10.00 / ISBN: 1-58322-029-1

CUTTING CORPORATE WELFARE
Ralph Nader
144 pages / $10.00 / ISBN: 1-58322-033-X

THE WTO: FIVE YEARS OF REASONS TO RESIST
CORPORATE GLOBALIZATION
Lori Wallach and Michelle Sforza
Introduction by Ralph Nader
80 pages / $5.95 / ISBN: 1-58322-035-6

THE CASE OF MUMIA ABU-JAMAL:
A LIFE IN THE BALANCE
Amnesty International
64 pages / $6.95 / ISBN: 1-58322-081-X

ISLANDS OF RESISTANCE:
PUERTO RICO, VIEQUES, AND U.S. POLICY
Mario Murillo
96 pages / $6.95 / ISBN: 1-58322-080-1

WEAPONS IN SPACE
Karl Grossman
96 pages / $6.95 / ISBN: 1-58322-044-5

10 REASONS TO ABOLISH THE IMF & WORLD BANK
Kevin Dahaner
104 pages / $6.95 / ISBN: 1-58322-464-5

SENT BY EARTH
Alice Walker
64 pages / $5.00 / ISBN: 1-58322-491-2

OPEN MEDIA BOOK

9-11
Noam Chomsky
128 pages / $8.95 / ISBN: 1-58322-489-0